William Cullen Bryant

A discourse on the life, character and genius of Washington Irving

Delivered before the New York historical society 1860

William Cullen Bryant

A discourse on the life, character and genius of Washington Irving
Delivered before the New York historical society 1860

ISBN/EAN: 9783337203474

Printed in Europe, USA, Canada, Australia, Japan

Cover: Foto ©ninafisch / pixelio.de

More available books at **www.hansebooks.com**

A DISCOURSE

ON THE

LIFE, CHARACTER AND GENIUS

OF

WASHINGTON IRVING,

DELIVERED BEFORE THE NEW YORK HISTORICAL SOCIETY,
AT THE ACADEMY OF MUSIC IN NEW YORK,
ON THE 3d OF APRIL, 1860.

BY

WILLIAM CULLEN BRYANT.

———•••———

NEW YORK:

G. P. PUTNAM, 115 NASSAU STREET,

1860.

A DISCOURSE

ON THE LIFE, CHARACTER, AND GENIUS OF WASHINGTON IRVING,

DELIVERED BEFORE THE NEW YORK HISTORICAL SOCIETY,

AT THE ACADEMY OF MUSIC, IN NEW YORK,

ON THE 3D OF APRIL, 1860,

BY WILLIAM CULLEN BRYANT.

WE have come together, my friends, on the birthday of an illustrious citizen of our republic; but so recent is his departure from among us, that our assembling is rather an expression of sorrow for his death than of congratulation that such a man was born into the world. His admirable writings, the beautiful products of his peculiar genius, remain, to be the enjoyment of the present and future generations. We keep the recollection of his amiable and blameless life, and his kindly manners, and for these we give thanks ; but the thought will force itself upon us that the light of his friendly eye is quenched, that we must no more hear his beloved voice, nor take his welcome hand. It is as if some genial year had just closed and left us in frost and gloom; its flowery spring, its leafy summer, its plenteous autumn, flown, never to return. Its gifts are strewn around us ; its harvests are in our garners; but its season of bloom, and warmth, and fruitfulness is past. We look around us and see that the sunshine, which filled the golden ear and tinged the reddening apple, brightens the earth no more.

Twelve years since, the task was assigned me to deliver the funeral eulogy of Thomas Cole, the great father of landscape painting in America, the artist who first taught the pencil to portray, with the boldness of nature, our wild forests and lake shores, our mountain regions and the borders of our majestic rivers. Five years later I was bidden to express, in such terms as I could command, the general sorrow which was felt for the death of Fenimore Cooper, equally great and equally the leader of his countrymen in a different walk of creative genius. Another grave has been opened, and he who has gone down to it, earlier than they in his labors and his fame, was, like them, foremost in the peculiar walk to which his genius attracted him. Cole was taken from us in the zenith of his manhood ; Cooper, when the sun of life had stooped from its meridian. In both instances the day was darkened by the cloud of death before the natural hour of its close ; but Irving was permitted to behold its light until, in the fulness of time and by the ordinary appointment of nature, it was carried below the horizon.

Washington Irving was born in New York, on the third of April, 1783, but a few days after the news of the treaty with Great Britain, acknowledging our independence, had been received, to the great contentment of the people. He opened his eyes to the light, therefore, just in the dawn of that Sabbath of peace which brought rest to the land after a weary seven years' war—just as the city of which he was a native, and the republic of which he was yet to be the ornament, were entering upon a career of greatness and prosperity of which those who inhabited them could scarce have dreamed. It seems fitting that one of the first births of the new peace, so welcome to the country, should be that of a genius as kindly and fruitful as peace itself, and destined to make the world better and happier by its gentle influences. In one respect, those who were born at that time had the advantage of those who are educated under the more vulgar influences of the present age. Before their eyes were placed, in the public actions of the men who achieved our revolution, noble examples of steady rectitude, magnanimous self-denial, and cheerful self-sacrifice for the sake of their country. Irving came into the world when these great and virtuous men were in the prime of their manhood, and passed his youth in the midst of that general reverence which gathered round them as they grew old.

William Irving, the father of the great author, was a native of Scotland—one of a race in which the instinct of veneration is strong—and a Scottish woman was employed as a nurse in his household. It is related that one day while she was walking in the street with her little charge, then five years old, she saw General Washington in a shop, and, entering, led up the boy, whom she presented as one to whom his name had been given. The general turned, laid his hand on the child's head, and gave him his smile and his blessing, little thinking that they were bestowed upon his future biographer. The gentle pressure of that hand Irving always remembered, and that blessing, he believed, attended him through life. Who shall say what power that recollection may have had in keeping him true to high and generous aims ?

At the time that Washington Irving was born, the city of New York contained scarcely more than twenty thousand inhabitants. During the war its population had probably diminished. The town was scarcely built up to Warren street ;

Broadway, a little beyond, was lost among grassy pastures and tilled fields ; the Park, in which now stands our City Hall, was an open common, and beyond it gleamed, in a hollow among the meadows, a little sheet of fresh water, the Kolch, from which a sluggish rivulet stole through the low grounds called Lispenard's Meadows, and following the course of what is now Canal street, entered the Hudson. With the exception of the little corner of the island below the present City Hall, the rural character of the whole region was unchanged, and the fresh air of the country entered New York at every street. The town at that time contained a mingled population, drawn from different countries ; but the descendants of the old Dutch settlers formed a large proportion of the inhabitants, and these preserved many of their peculiar customs, and had not ceased to use the speech of their ancestors at their firesides. Many of them lived in the quaint old houses, built of small yellow bricks from Holland, with their notched gable-ends on the streets, which have since been swept away with the language of those who built them.

In the surrounding country, along its rivers and beside its harbors, and in many parts far inland, the original character of the Dutch settlements was still less changed. Here they read their Bibles and said their prayers and listened to sermons in the ancestral tongue. Remains of this language yet linger in a few neighborhoods ; but in most, the common schools, and the irruptions of the Yankee race, and the growth of a population newly derived from Europe, have stifled the ancient utterances of New Amsterdam. I remember that twenty years since the market people of Bergen chattered Dutch in the steamers which brought them in the early morning to New York. I remember also that, about ten years before, there were families in the westernmost towns of Massachusetts where Dutch was still the household tongue, and matrons of the English stock, marrying into them, were laughed at for speaking it so badly.

It will be readily inferred that the isolation in which the use of a language, strange to the rest of the country, placed these people, would form them to a character of peculiar simplicity, in which there was a great deal that was quaint and not a little that would appear comic to their neighbors of the Anglo-Saxon stock. It was among such a population, friendly and hospitable, wearing their faults on the outside, and living in homely comfort on their fertile and ample acres, that the boyhood and early youth of Irving were passed. He began, while yet a stripling, to wander about the surrounding country; for the love of rambling was the most remarkable peculiarity of that period of his life. He became, as he himself writes, familiar with all the neighboring places famous in history or fable, knew every spot where a murder or a robbery had been committed or a ghost seen ; strolled into the villages, noted their customs and talked with their sages, a welcome guest, doubtless, with his kindly and ingenuous manners and the natural playful turn of his conversation.

I dwell upon these particulars because they help to show here how the mind of Irving was trained, and by what process he made himself master of the materials afterward wrought into the forms we so much admire. It was in these rambles that his strong love of nature was awakened and nourished. Those who only know the island of New York as it now is, see few traces of the beauty it wore before it was levelled and smoothed from side to side for the builder. Immediately without the little town, it was charmingly diversified with heights and hollows, groves alternating with sunny openings, shining tracks of rivulets, quiet country-seats with trim gardens, broad avenues of

trees, and lines of pleached hawthorn hedges. I came to New
York in 1825, and I well recollect how much I admired the
shores of the Hudson above Canal street, where the dark rocks
jutted far out in the water, with little bays between, above
which drooped forest trees overrun with wild vines. No less
beautiful were the shores of the East River, where the orchards
of the Stuyvesant estate reached to cliffs beetling over the
water, and still further on were inlets between rocky banks
bristling with red cedars. Some idea of this beauty may be
formed from looking at what remains of the natural shore of
New York island where the tides of the East River rush to and
fro by the rocky verge of Jones's Wood.

Here wandered Irving in his youth, and allowed the aspect of
that nature which he afterward portrayed so well to engrave
itself on his heart ; but his excursions were not confined to this
island. He became familiar with the banks of the Hudson, the
extraordinary beauty of which he was the first to describe. He
made acquaintance with the Dutch neighborhoods sheltered by
its hills, Nyack, Haverstraw, Sing Sing and Sleepy Hollow, and
with the majestic Highlands beyond. His rambles in another
direction led him to ancient Communipaw, lying in its quiet
recess by New York bay ; to the then peaceful Gowanus, now
noisy with the passage of visitors to Greenwood and thronged
with funerals ; to Hoboken, Horsimus and Paulus Hook, which
has since become a city. A ferry-boat dancing on the rapid
tides took him over to Brooklyn, now our flourishing and
beautiful neighbor city ; then a cluster of Dutch farms, whose
possessors lived in broad, low houses, with stoops in front, over-
shadowed by trees.

The generation with whom Irving grew up read the " Spectator " and the " Rambler," the essays and tales of Mackenzie and

those of Goldsmith ; the novels of the day were those of Richardson, Fielding and Smollett ; the religious world were occupied with the pages of Hannah More, fresh from the press, and with the writings of Doddridge ; politicians sought their models of style and reasoning in the speeches of Burke and the writings of Mackintosh and Junius. These were certainly masters of whom no pupil needed to be ashamed, but it can hardly be said that the style of Irving was formed in the school of any of them. His father's library was enriched with authors of the Elizabethan age, and he delighted, we are told, in reading Chaucer and Spenser. The elder of these great poets might have taught him the art of heightening his genial humor with poetic graces, and from both he might have learned a freer mastery over his native English than the somewhat formal taste of that day encouraged. Cowper's poems, at that time, were in everybody's hands, and if his father had not those of Burns, we must believe that he was no Scotchman. I think we may fairly infer that if the style of Irving took a bolder range than was allowed in the way of writing which prevailed when he was a youth, it was owing, in a great degree, to his studies in the poets, and especially in those of the earlier English literature.

He owed little to the schools, though he began to attend them early. His first instructions were given when he was between four and six years old, by Mrs. Ann Kilmaster, at her school in Ann street, who seems to have had some difficulty in getting him through the alphabet. In 1789, he was transferred to a school in Fulton street, then called Partition street, kept by Benjamin Romaine, who had been a soldier in the Revolution —a sensible man and a good disciplinarian, but probably an indifferent scholar—and here he continued till he was fourteen years of age. He was a favorite with the master, but preferred

reading to regular study. At ten years of age he delighted in
the wild tales of Ariosto, as translated by Hoole ; at eleven, he
was deep in books of voyages and travels, which he took to
school and read by stealth. At that time he composed with
remarkable ease and fluency, and exchanged tasks with the other
boys, writing their compositions, while they solved his problems
in arithmetic, which he detested. At the age of thirteen he
tried his hand at composing a play, which was performed by
children at a friend's house, and of which he afterward forgot
every part, even the title.

Romaine gave up teaching in 1797, and in that year Irving
entered a school kept in Beekman street, by Jonathan Irish,
probably the most accomplished of his instructors. He left this
school in March, 1798, but continued for a time to receive pri-
vate lessons from the same teacher, at home. Dr. Francis, in
his pleasant reminiscences of Irving's early life, speaks of him as
preparing to enter Columbia College, and as being prevented by
the state of his health ; but it is certain that an indifference to
the acquisition of learning had taken possession of him at that
age, which he afterward greatly regretted.

At the age of sixteen he entered his name as a student at law
in the office of Josiah Ogden Hoffman, an eminent advocate,
who, in later life, became a judge in one of our principal tribu-
nals. It was while engaged in his professional studies that he
made his first appearance as an author. I should have mentioned, among the circumstances that favored the unfolding of
his literary capacities, that two of his elder brothers were men
of decided literary tastes, William Irving, some seventeen years
his senior, and Dr. Peter Irving, who, in the year 1802, founded
a daily paper in New York, at a time when a daily paper was
not, as now, an enterprise requiring a large outlay of capital,

but an experiment that might be tried and abandoned with little risk. Dr. Irving established the "Morning Chronicle," and his younger brother contributed a series of essays, bearing the signature of Jonathan Oldstyle, of which Mr. Duyckinck, whose judgment I willingly accept, says that they show how early he acquired the style which so much charms us in his later writings.

In 1804, having reached the age of twenty-one, Irving, alarmed by an increasing weakness of the chest, visited Europe for the sake of his health. He sailed directly to the south of France, landed at Bordeaux in May, and passed two months in Genoa, where he embarked for Messina, in search of a softer climate than any to be found on the Italian peninsula. While at Messina, he saw the fleet of Nelson sweeping by that port on its way to fight the great naval battle of Trafalgar. He made the tour of Sicily, and crossing from Palermo to Naples, proceeded to Rome. Here he formed the acquaintance of Washington Allston, who was then entering on a career of art as extraordinary as that of Irving in literature. With Allston he made long rambles in the picturesque neighborhood of that old city, visited the galleries of its palaces and villas, and studied their works of art with a delight that rose to enthusiasm. He thought of the dry pursuit of the law which awaited his return to America, and for which he had no inclination, and almost determined to be a painter. Allston encouraged him in this disposition, and together they planned the scheme of a life devoted to the pursuit of art. It was fortunate for the world that, as Irving reflected on the matter, doubts arose in his mind which tempered his enthusiasm, and led him to a different destiny. The two friends separated, each to take his own way to renown— Allston to become one of the greatest of painters, and Irving to take his place among the greatest of authors. Leaving Italy, Irving passed through Switzerland to France, resided in Paris several months, travelled through Flanders and Holland, went to England, and returned to his native country in 1806, after an absence of two years.

At the close of the year he was admitted to practice as an attorney-at-law. He opened an office, but it could not be said that he ever became a practitioner. He began the year 1807 with the earliest of those literary labors which have won him the admiration of the world. On the 24th of January appeared, in the form of a small pamphlet, the first number of a periodical entitled "Salmagundi," the joint production of himself, his brother William, and James K. Paulding. The elder brother contributed the poetry, with hints and outlines for some of the essays, but nearly all the prose was written by the two younger associates.

William Irving, however, had talent enough to have taken a more important part in the work. He was a man of wit, well educated, well informed, and the author of many clever things written for the press, in a vein of good natured satire and published without his name. He was held in great esteem on account of his personal character, and had great weight in Congress, of which he was for some years a member.*

When "Salmagundi" appeared, the quaint old Dutch town in which Irving was born had become transformed to a comparatively gay metropolis. Its population of twenty thousand souls had enlarged to more than eighty thousand, although its aristocratic class had yet their residences in what seems now to us the narrow space between the Battery and Wall street. The

* See a brief but well written memoir of William Irving by Dr. Berrian.

modes and fashions of Europe were imported fresh and fresh. "Salmagundi" speaks of leather breeches as all the rage for a morning dress, and flesh-colored smalls for an evening party. Gay equipages dashed through the streets. A new theatre had risen in Park Row, on the boards of which Cooper, one of the finest declaimers, was performing to crowded houses. The churches had multiplied faster than the places of amusement; other public buildings of a magnificence hitherto unknown, including our present City Hall, had been erected ; Tammany Hall, fresh from the hands of the builder, overlooked the Park. We began to affect a taste for pictures, and the rooms of Michael Paff, the famous German picture-dealer in Broadway, were a favorite lounge for such connoisseurs as we then had, who amused themselves with making him talk of Michael Angelo. Ballston Springs were the great fashionable watering-place of the country, to which resorted the planters of the South with splendid equipages and troops of shining blacks in livery.

"Salmagundi" satirized the follies and ridiculed the humors of the time with great prodigality of wit and no less exuberance of good nature. In form it resembles the "Tattler," and that numerous brood of periodical papers to which the success of the "Tattler" and "Spectator" gave birth; but it is in no sense an imitation. Its gaiety is its own; its style of humor is not that of Addison nor Goldsmith, though it has all the genial spirit of theirs; nor is it borrowed from any other writer. It is far more frolicsome and joyous, yet tempered by a native gracefulness. "Salmagundi" was manifestly written without the fear of criticism before the eyes of the authors, and to this sense of perfect freedom in the exercise of their genius the charm is probably owing which makes us still read it with so much delight. Irving never seemed to place much value on the part he contributed to this work, yet I doubt whether he ever excelled some of those papers in *Salmagundi* which bear the most evident marks of his style, and Paulding, though he has since acquired a reputation by his other writings, can hardly be said to have written anything better than the best of those which are ascribed to his pen.

Just before *Salmagundi* appeared, several of the authors who gave the literature of England its present character had begun to write. For five years the quarterly issues of the " Edinburgh Review," then in the most brilliant period of its existence, had been before the public. Hazlitt had taken his place among the authors, and John Foster had published his essays. Of the poets, Rogers, Campbell and Moore were beginning to be popular ; Wordsworth had published his Lyrical Ballads, Scott, his Lay of the Last Ministrel, Southey, his Madoc, and Joanna Baillie two volumes of her plays. In this revival of the creative power in literature it is pleasant to see that our own country took part, contributing a work of a character as fresh and original as any they produced on the other side of the Atlantic.

Nearly two years afterward, in the autumn of 1809, appeared in the " Evening Post," addressed to the humane, an advertisement requesting information concerning a small elderly gentleman named Knickerbocker, dressed in a black coat and cocked hat, who had suddenly left his lodgings at the Columbian Hotel in Mulberry street, and had not been heard of afterward. In the beginning of November, a "Traveller" communicated to the same journal the information that he had seen a person answering to this description, apparently fatigued with his journey, resting by the road-side a little north of Kingsbridge. Ten days later Seth Handaside, the landlord of the Columbian Hotel, gave notice, through the same journal, that he had found in the missing gentleman's chamber " a curious kind of written book," which he should print by way of reimbursing himself for what his lodger owed him. In December following, Inskeep and Bradford, booksellers, published "Diedrich Knicker-bocker's History of New York."

"Salmagundi" had prepared the public to receive this work with favor, and Seth Handaside had no reason to regret having undertaken its publication. I recollect well its early and imme-diate popularity. I was then a youth in college, and having committed to memory a portion of it to repeat as a declamation before my class, I was so overcome with laughter, when I [1] appeared on the floor, that I was unable to proceed, and drew upon myself the rebuke of the tutor.

I have just read this "History of New York" over again, and I found myself no less delighted than when I first turned its pages in my early youth. When I compare it with other works of wit and humor of a similar length, I find that, unlike most of them, it carries forward the reader to the conclusion without weariness or satiety, so unsought, spontaneous, self-sug-gested are the wit and the humor. The author makes us laugh, because he can no more help it than we can help laughing. Scott, in one of his letters, compared the humor of this work to that of Swift. The rich vein of Irving's mirth is of a quality quite distinct from the dry drollery of Swift, but they have this in common, that they charm by the utter absence of effort, and this was probably the ground of Scott's remark. A critic in the "London Quarterly," some years after its appearance, spoke of it as a "tantalizing book," on account of his inability to under-stand what he called "the point of many of the allusions in this political satire." I fear he must have been one of those respect-able persons who find it difficult to understand a joke unless it be accompanied with a commentary opening and explaining it

to the humblest capacity. Scott found no such difficulty.
" Our sides," he says, in a letter to Mr. Brevoort, a friend of
Irving, written just after he had read the book, "are absolutely
sore with laughing." The mirth of the " History of New
York " is of the most transparent sort, and the author, even in
the later editions, judiciously abstained from any attempt to
make it more intelligible by notes.

I find in this work more manifest traces than in his other
writings of what Irving owed to the earlier authors in our language. The quaint poetic coloring, and often the phraseology,
betray the disciple of Chaucer and Spenser. We are conscious
of a flavor of the olden time, as of a racy wine of some rich
vintage—

"Cooled a long age in the deep-delvèd earth.

I will not say that there are no passages in this work which
are not worthy of their context ; that we do not sometimes
meet with phraseology which we could wish changed, that the
wit does not sometimes run wild and drop here and there a jest
which we could willingly spare. We forgive, we overlook, we
forget all this as we read, in consideration of the entertainment
we have enjoyed, and of that which beckons us onward in the
next page. Of all mock-heroic works, " Knickerbocker's History of New York " is the gayest, the airiest, and the least tire-
some.

In 1848 Mr. Irving issued an edition of this work, to which
he prefixed what he called an " Apology," intended in part as
an answer to those who thought he had made too free with the
names of our old Dutch families. To speak frankly, I do not
much wonder that the descendants of the original founders of
New Amsterdam should have hardly known whether to laugh

or look grave on finding the names of their ancestors, of whom they never thought but with respect, now connected with ludicrous associations, by a wit of another race. In one of his excellent historical discourses Mr. Verplanck had gently complained of this freedom, expressing himself, as he said, more in sorrow than in anger. Even the sorrow, I believe, must have long since wholly passed away, when it is seen how little Irving's pleasantries have detracted from the honor paid to the early history of our city—at all events, I do not see how it could survive Irving's good-humored and graceful Apology.

It was not long after the publication of the "History of New York" that Irving abandoned the profession of law, for which he had so decided a distaste as never to have fully tried his capacity for pursuing it. Two of his brothers were engaged in commerce, and they received him as a silent partner. He did not, however, renounce his literary occupations. He wrote, in 1810, a memoir of Campbell, the poet, prefaced to an edition of the writings of that author, which appeared in Philadelphia ; and in 1813 and the following year, employed himself as editor of the "Analectic Magazine," published in the same city ; making the experiment of his talent for a vocation to which men of decided literary tastes in this country are strongly inclined to betake themselves. Those who remember this magazine cannot have forgotten that it was a most entertaining miscellany, partly compiled from English publications, mostly periodicals, and partly made up of contributions of some of our own best writers. Paulding wrote for it a series of biographical accounts of the naval commanders of the United States, which added greatly to its popularity ; and Verplanck contributed memoirs of Commodore Stewart and General Scott, Barlow, the poet, and other distinguished Americans, which were received with favor.

The Life of Campbell, with the exception perhaps of some less important contributions to the magazine, is the only published work of Irving between the appearance of the "History of New York," in 1809, and that of the "Sketch Book," in 1819.

It was during this interval that an event took place which had a marked influence on Irving's future life, affected the character of his writings, and, now that the death of both parties allow it to be spoken of without reserve, gives a peculiar interest to his personal history. He became attached to a young lady whom he was to have married. She died unwedded, in the flower of her age ; there was a sorrowful leave-taking between her and her lover, as the grave was about to separate them on the eve of what should have been her bridal ; and Irving, ever after, to the close of his life, tenderly and faithfully cherished her memory. In one of the biographical notices published immediately after Irving's death, an old, well-worn copy of the Bible is spoken of, which was kept lying on the table in his chamber, within reach of his bedside, bearing her name on the title page in a delicate female hand—a relic which we may presume to have been his constant companion. Those who are fond of searching, in the biographies of eminent men, for the circumstances which determined the bent of their genius, find in this sad event, and the cloud it threw over the hopeful and cheerful period of early manhood, an explanation of the transition from the unbounded playfulness of the "History of New York" to the serious, tender and meditative vein of the "Sketch Book."

In 1815, soon after our second peace with Great Britain, Irving sailed again for Europe, and fixed himself at Liverpool, where a branch of the large commercial house to which he belonged was established. His old love of rambling returned upon him ; he wandered first into Wales, and over some of the finest counties of England, and then northward to the sterner region of the Scottish Highlands. His memoir of Campbell had procured him the acquaintance and friendship of that poet. Campbell gave him, more than a year after his arrival in England, a letter of introduction to Scott, who, already acquainted with him by his writings, welcomed him warmly to Abbotsford, and made him his friend for life. Scott sent a special message to Campbell, thanking him for having made him known to Irving. " He is one of the best and pleasantest acquaintances," said Scott, " that I have made this many a day."

In the same year that he visited Abbotsford his brothers failed. The changes which followed the peace of 1815, swept away their fortunes and his together, and he was now to begin the world anew.

In 1819, he began to publish the Sketch Book. It was written in England and sent over to New York, where it was issued by Van Winkle, in octavo numbers, containing from seventy to a hundred pages. In the preface he remarked that he was " unsettled in his abode," that he had "his cares and vicissitudes," and could not, therefore, give these papers the " tranquil attention necessary to finished composition." Several of them were copied with praise in the London " Literary Gazette," and an intimation was conveyed to the author, that some person in London was about to publish them entire. He preferred to do this himself, and accordingly offered the work to the famous bookseller, Murray. Murray was slow in giving the matter his attention, and Irving, after a reasonable delay, wrote to ask that the copy which he had left with him might be returned. It was sent back with a note, pleading excess of occupation, the great cross of all eminent booksellers, and alleging the " want of scope in the nature of the work," as a reason for declining it. This was discouraging, but Irving had the enterprise to print the first volume in London, at his own risk. It was issued by John Miller, and was well received, but in a month afterward the publisher failed. Immediately Sir Walter Scott came to London and saw Murray, who allowed himself to be persuaded, the more easily, doubtless, on account of the partial success of the first volume, that the work had more " scope" than he supposed, and purchased the copyright of both volumes for two hundred pounds, which he afterward liberally raised to four hundred.

Whoever compares the Sketch Book with the History of New York might at first, perhaps, fail to recognize it as the work of the same hand, so much graver and more thoughtful is the strain in which it is written. A more attentive examination, however, shows that the humor in the lighter parts is of the same peculiar and original cast, wholly unlike that of any author who ever wrote, a humor which Mr. Dana happily characterized as " a fanciful playing with common things, and here and there beautiful touches, till the ludicrous becomes half picturesque." Yet one cannot help perceiving that the author's spirit had been sobered since he last appeared before the public, as if the shadow of a great sorrow had fallen upon it. The greater number of the papers are addressed to our deeper sympathies, and some of them, as, for example, the Broken Heart, the Widow and Her Son, and Rural Funerals, dwell upon the saddest themes. Only in two of them—Rip Van Winkle and the Legend of Sleepy Hollow—does he lay the reins loose on the neck of his frolicsome fancy, and allow it to dash forward without restraint ; and these rank among the most delightful and popular tales ever written. In our country they have been read, I believe, by nearly everybody who can read at all.

The "Sketch Book," and the two succeeding works of Irving, "Bracebridge Hall" and the "Tales of a Traveller," abound with agreeable pictures of English life, seen under favorable lights and sketched with a friendly pencil. ⌈Let me say here, that it was not to pay court to the English that he thus described them and their country ; it was because he could not describe them otherwise. It was the instinct of his mind to attach itself to the contemplation of the good and the beautiful, wherever he found them, and to turn away from the sight of what was evil, misshapen and hateful. His was not a nature to pry for faults, or disabuse the world of good-natured mistakes ; he looked for virtue, love and truth among men, and thanked God that he found them in such large measure. If there are touches of satire in his writings, he is the best-natured and most amiable of satirists, amiable beyond Horace ; and in his irony—for there is a vein of playful irony running through many of his works—there is no tinge of bitterness.

I rejoice, for my part, that we have had such a writer as Irving to bridge over the chasm between the two great nations —that an illustrious American lived so long in England, and was so much beloved there, and sought so earnestly to bring the people of the two countries to a better understanding with each other, and to wean them from the animosities of narrow minds. I am sure that there is not a large-minded and large-hearted man in all our country who can read over the " Sketch Book " and the other writings of Irving, and disown one of the magnanimous sentiments they express with regard to England, or desire to abate the glow of one of his warm and cheerful pictures of English life. Occasions will arise, no doubt, for saying some things in a less accommodating spirit, and there are men enough on both sides of the Atlantic who can say them ; but

Irving was not sent into the world on that errand. A different
work was assigned him in the very structure of his mind, and
the endowments of his heart—a work of peace and brotherhood,
and I will say for him that he nobly performed it.

Let me pause here to speak of what I believe to have been
the influence of the "Sketch Book" upon American literature.
At the time it appeared the periodical lists of new American
publications were extremely meagre, and consisted, to a great
extent, of occasional pamphlets and dissertations on the ques-
tions of the day. The works of greater pretension were, for
the most part, crudely and languidly made up, and destined to
be little read. A work like the "Sketch Book," welcomed on
both sides of the Atlantic, showed the possibility of an American author acquiring a fame bounded only by the limits of his
own language, and gave an example of the qualities by which it
might be won. Within two years afterward we had Cooper's
"Spy" and Dana's "Idle Man;" the press of our country began,
by degrees, to teem with works composed with a literary skill
and a spirited activity of intellect until then little known among
us. Every year the assertion that we had no literature of our
own became less and less true : and now, when we look over a
list of new works by native authors, we find, with an astonish-
ment amounting almost to alarm, that the most voracious
devourer of books must despair of being able to read half those
which make a fair claim upon his attention. It was since 1819
that the great historians of our country, whose praise is in the
mouths of all the nations, began to write. One of them built
up the fabric of his fame long after Irving appeared as an
author, and slept with Herodotus two years before Irving's
death ; another of the band lives yet to be the ornament of the
association before which I am called to speak, and is framing

the annals of his country into a work for future ages. Within that period has arisen among us the class who hold vast multitudes spell-bound in motionless attention by public discourses, the most perfect of their kind, such as make the fame of Everett. Within that period our theologians have learned to write with the elegance and vivacity of the essayists. We had but one novelist before the era of the "Sketch Book;" their number is now beyond enumeration by any but a professed catalogue-maker, and many of them are read in every cultivated form of human speech. Those whom we acknowledge as our poets—one of whom is the special favorite of our brothers in language who dwell beyond sea—appeared in the world of letters and won its attention after Irving had become famous. We have wits, and humorists, and amusing essayists, authors of some of the airiest and most graceful compositions of the present century, and we owe them to the new impulse given to our literature in 1819. I look abroad on these stars of our literary firmament—some crowded together with their minute points of light in a galaxy—some standing apart in glorious constellations; I recognize Arcturus, and Orion, and Perseus, and the glittering jewels of the Southern Crown, and the Pleiades shedding sweet influences; but the Evening Star, the soft and serene light that glowed in their van, the precursor of them all, has sunk · below the horizon. The spheres, meantime, perform their appointed courses; the same motion which lifted them up to the mid-sky bears them onward to their setting; and they, too, like their bright leader, must soon be carried by it below the earth.

Irving went to Paris in 1820, where he passed the remainder of the year and part of the next, and where he became acquainted with the poet Moore, who frequently mentions him

2

in his Diary. Moore and he were much in each other's company and the poet has left on record an expression of his amazement at the rapidity with which "Bracebridge Hall" was composed—one hundred and thirty pages in ten days. The winter of 1822 found him in Dresden. In that year was published "Bracebridge Hall," the groundwork of which is a charming description of country life in England, interspersed with narratives, the scene of which is laid in other countries. Of these, the Norman tale of "Annette Delarbre" seems to me the most beautiful and affecting thing of its kind in all his works ; so beautiful, indeed, that I can hardly see how he who has once read it can resist the desire to read it again. In "Bracebridge Hall" we have the Stout Gentleman, full of certain minute paintings of familiar objects, where not a single touch is thrown in that does not heighten the comic effect of the narrative. If I am not greatly mistaken, the most popular novelists of the day have learned from this pattern the skill with which they have wrought up some of their most striking passages, both grave and gay. In composing "Bracebridge Hall," Irving showed that he had not forgotten his native country ; and in the pleasant tale of Dolph Heyleger he went back to the banks of that glorious river beside which he was born.

In 1823, Irving, still a wanderer, returned to Paris, and in the year following gave the world his "Tales of a Traveller." Murray, in the meantime, had become fully weaned from the notion that Irving's writings lacked the quality which he called "scope," for he had paid a thousand guineas for the copyright of "Bracebridge Hall," and now offered fifteen hundred pounds for the "Tales of a Traveller," which Irving accepted. "He might have had two thousand," says Moore, but this assembly will not, I hope, think the worse of him, if it be acknowledged that

the world contained men who were sharper than he at driving a
bargain.   The "Tales of a Traveller" are most remarkable for
their second part, entitled "Buckthorne and his Friends," in which
the author introduces us to literary life in its various aspects, as he
had observed it in London, and to the relations in which authors
at that time stood to the booksellers.   His sketches of the different personages are individual, characteristic and diverting, yet
with what a kindly pencil they are all drawn!   His good nature
overspreads and harmonizes everything, like the warm atmosphere which so much delights us in a painting.

Irving, still "unsettled in his abode," passed the winter of
1825 in the south of France.   When you are in that region
you see the snowy summits of the Spanish Pyrenees looking
down upon you ; Spanish visitors frequent the watering-places ;
Spanish pedlers, in their handsome costume, offer you the
fabrics of Barcelona and Valencia ; Spanish peasants come to
the fairs ; the traveller feels himself almost in Spain already,
and is haunted by the desire of visiting that remarkable country.
To Spain, Irving went in the latter part of the year, invited by
our Minister at Madrid, Alexander H. Everett, at the sugges-
tion of Mr. Rich, the American Consul, an industrious and
intelligent collector of Spanish works relating to America.   His
errand was to translate into English the documents relating to
the discovery and early history of our Continent, collected by
the research of Navarrete.   He passed the winter of 1826 at
the Spanish capital, as the guest of Mr. Rich ; the following
season took him to Granada, and he lingered awhile in that
beautiful region, profusedly watered by the streams that break
from the Snowy Ridge.   In 1827, he again visited the South of
Spain, gathering materials for his "Life of Columbus," which,
immediately after his arrival in Spain, he had determined to write,

instead of translating the documents of Navarrete. In Spain
he began and finished that work, after having visited the places
associated with the principal events in the life of his hero.
Murray was so well satisfied with its "scope" that he gave him
three thousand guineas for the copyright, and laid it before the
public in 1828. Like the other works of Irving's, it was published here at the same time as in London.

The "Life and Voyages of Christopher Columbus" placed
Irving among the historians, for the biography of that great dis-
coverer is a part, and a remarkable part, of the history of the
world. Of what was strictly and simply personal in his adventures, much, of course, has passed into irremediable oblivion; what
was both personal and historical is yet outstanding above the
shadow that has settled upon the rest. The work of Irving
was at once in everybody's hands and eagerly read. Navarrete
vouched for its historical accuracy and completeness. Jeffrey
declared that no work could ever take its place. It was written
with a strong love of the subject, and to this it owes much of
its power over the reader. Columbus was one of those who,
with all their faculties occupied by one great idea, and bent
on making it a practical reality, are looked upon as crazed, and
pitied and forgotten if they fail, but if they succeed are vene-
rated as the glory of their age. The poetic elements of his character and history, the grandeur and mystery of his design, his
prophetic sagacity, his hopeful and devout courage, and his dis-
regard of the ridicule of meaner intellects, took a strong hold
on the mind of Irving, and formed the inspiration of the work.

Mr. Duyckinck gives, on the authority of one who knew
Irving intimately, an instructive anecdote relating to the "Life
of Columbus." When the work was nearly finished it was put
into the hands of Lieutenant Slidell Mackenzie, himself an agree-

able writer, then on a visit to Spain, who read it with a view of giving a critical opinion of its merits. "It is quite perfect," said he, on returning the manuscript, "except the style, and that is unequal." The remark made such an impression on the mind of the author that he wrote over the whole narrative with the view of making the style more uniform, but he afterward thought that he had not improved it.

In this I have no doubt that Irving was quite right, and that it would have been better if he had never touched the work after he had brought it to the state which satisfied his individual judgment. An author can scarce commit a greater error than to alter what he writes, except when he has a clear perception that the alteration is for the better, and can make it with as hearty a confidence in himself as he felt in giving the work its first shape. What strikes me as an occasional defect in the "Life of Columbus" is this elaborate uniformity of style— a certain prismatic coloring in passages where absolute simplicity would have satisfied us better. It may well be supposed that Irving originally wrote some parts of the work with the quiet plainness of a calm relater of facts, and others, with the spirit and fire of one who had become warmed with his subject, and this probably gave occasion to what was said of the inequality of the style. The attempt to elevate the diction of the simpler portions, we may suppose, marred what Irving afterward perceived had really been one of the merits of the work.

In the spring of 1829, Irving made another visit to the south of Spain, collecting materials from which he afterward composed some of his most popular works. When the traveller now visits Granada and is taken to the Alhambra, his guide will say, "Here is one of the curiosities of the place ; this is the chamber occupied by Washington Irving," and he will show an

apartment, from the windows of which you have a view of the
glorious valley of the Genil, with the mountain peaks overlook-
ing it, and hear the murmur of many mountain brooks at once,
as they hurry to the plain. In July of the same year, he
repaired to London, where he was to act as Secretary of the
American Legation. We had at that time certain controver-
sies with the British government which were the subject of nego-
tiation. Irving took great interest in these, and in some letters which I saw at the time, stated the points in dispute at
considerable length and with admirable method and perspicuity.
In London he published his " Chronicles of the Conquest of
Granada," one of the most delightful of his works, an exact history, for such_it is admitted to be by those who have searched
most carefully the ancient records of Spain, yet so full of personal incident, so diversified with surprising turns of fortune,
and these wrought up with such picturesque effect, that, to use
an expression of Pope, a young lady might read it by mistake
for a romance. In 1831, he gave the world another work on
Spanish history, the " Voyages of the Companions of Columbus," and in the year following the " Alhambra," which is another
" Sketch Book," with the scenes laid in Spain.

While in Spain, Irving had planned a Life of Cortez, the Con-
queror of Mexico, and collected the facts from which it was to
be written. When, afterward, he had actually begun the composition of the work, he happened to learn that Prescott
designed to write the " History of the Mexican Conquest," and
immediately he desisted. It was his intention to interweave
with the narrative, descriptions of the ancient customs of the
aborigines, such as their modes of warfare and their gorgeous
pageants, by way of relief to the sanguinary barbarities of the
Conquest. He saw what rich materials of the picturesque these

opened to him, and if he had accomplished his plan, he would probably have produced one of his most popular works.

In 1832, Irving returned to New York. He returned, after an absence of seventeen years, to find his native city doubled in population ; its once quiet waters alive with sails and furrowed by steamers passing to and fro, its wharves crowded with masts ; the heights which surround it, and which he remembered wild and solitary and lying in forest, now crowned with stately country seats, or with dwellings clustered in villages, and everywhere the activity and bustle of a prosperous and hopeful people. And he, too, how had he returned ? The young and comparatively obscure author, whose works had only found here and there a reader in England, had achieved a fame as wide as the civilized world. All the trophies he had won in this field he brought home to lay at the feet of his country. Meanwhile all the country was moved to meet him ; the rejoicing was universal that one who had represented us so illustriously abroad was henceforth to live among us.

Irving hated public dinners, but he was forced to accept one pressed upon him by his enthusiastic countrymen. It was given at the City Hotel on the 30th of May, Chancellor Kent presiding, and the most eminent citizens of New York assembled at the table. I remember the accounts of this festivity reaching me as I was wandering in Illinois, hovering on the skirts of the Indian war, in a region now populous, but then untilled and waste, and I could only write to Irving and ask leave to add my voice to the general acclamation. In his address at the dinner, Chancellor Kent welcomed the historian of New Amsterdam back to his native city, and Irving, in reply, poured forth his heart in the warmest expressions of delight at finding himself again among his countrymen and kindred, in a land of sunshine and freedom and hope. " I am asked," he said, " how long I mean to remain here. They know little of my heart who can ask me this question. I answer, as long as I live."

The instinct of rambling, had not, however, forsaken him. In the summer after his return he made a journey to the country west of the Mississippi, in company with Mr. Ellsworth, a commissioner intrusted with the removal of certain Indian tribes, and roamed over wild regions, then the hunting-grounds of the savage, but into which the white man has since brought his plough and his herds. He did not publish his account of this journey until 1835, when it appeared as the first volume of the " Crayon Miscellany," under the title of a " Tour on the Prairies." In this work the original West is described as Irving knew how to describe it, and the narrative is in that vein of easy gaiety peculiar to his writings. " Abbotsford and Newstead Abbey " formed the second volume of the " Crayon Miscellany," and to these he afterward added another, entitled " Legends of the Conquest of Spain."

In 1836, he published " Astoria ; or, Anecdotes of an Enterprise beyond the Rocky Mountains ;" a somewhat curious example of literary skill. A voluminous commercial correspondence was the dull ore of the earth which he refined and wrought into symmetry and splendor. Irving reduced to a regular narrative the events to which it referred, bringing out the picturesque whenever he found it, and enlivening the whole with touches of his native humor. His nephew, Pierre M. Irving, lightened his labor materially by examining and collating the letters and making memoranda of their contents. In 1837, he prepared for the press the " Adventures of Captain Bonneville, of the United States Army, in the Rocky Mountains and the Far West." He had the manuscript journal of Bonneville before him, but the hand of Irving is apparent in every sentence.

About the time that this work appeared, Irving was drawn into the only public controversy in which, so far as I know, he ever engaged. William Leggett then conducted a weekly periodical entitled the "Plaindealer," remarkable both for its ability and its love of disputation. It attacked Mr. Irving for altering a line or two in one of my poems, with a view of making it less offensive to English readers, and for writing a preface to the American edition of his "Tour on the Prairies," full of professions of love for his country, which were studiously omitted from the English edition. From these circumstances the "Plaindealer" drew an inference unfavorable to Irving's sincerity.

I should here mention, and I hope I may do it without much egotism, that when a volume of my poems was published here in the year 1832, Mr. Verplanck had the kindness to send a copy of it to Irving, desiring him to find a publisher for it in England. This he readily engaged to do, though wholly unacquainted with me, and offered the volume to Murray. "Poetry does not sell at present," said Murray, and declined it. A bookseller in Bond street, named Andrews, undertook its publication, but required that Irving should introduce it with a preface of his own. He did so, speaking of my verses in such terms as would naturally command for them the attention of the public, and allowing his name to be placed in the title-page as the editor. The edition, in consequence, found a sale. It happened, however, that the publisher objected to two lines in a poem called the "Song of Marion's Men." One of them was

"The British soldier trembles,"

and Irving good-naturedly consented that it should be altered to

2*

"The foeman trembles in his camp."

The other alteration was of a similar character.

To the accusations of the " Plaindealer," Irving replied with a mingled spirit and dignity which almost makes us regret that his faculties were not oftener roused into energy by such collisions, or, at least, that he did not sometimes employ his pen on contro-verted points. He fully vindicated himself in both instances, showing that he had made the alterations in my poem from a simple desire to do me service, and that with regard to the " Tour on the Prairies," he had sent a manuscript copy of it to England for publication, at the same time that he sent another to the printer here, and that it would have been an absurdity to address the English edition to the American public. But as this was the first time that he had appeared before his country-men as an author since his return from Europe, it was but pro-per that he should express to them the feelings awakened by their generous welcome.   "These feelings," he said, "were genuine, and were not expressed with half the warmth with which they were entertained ;" an assertion which every reader, I believe, was disposed to receive literally.

In his answer to the " Plaindealer," some allusions were made to me which seemed to imply that I had taken part in this attack upon him. To remove the impression, I sent a note to the " Plaindealer " for publication, in which I declared in sub-stance that I never had complained of the alterations of my poem—that though they were not such as I should have made, I was certain they were made with the kindest intentions, and that I had no feeling toward Mr. Irving but gratitude for the service he had rendered me. The explanation was graciously accepted, and in a brief note, printed in the " Plaindealer," Irving pronounced my acquittal.

Several papers were written by Irving in 1839 and the following year, for the "Knickerbocker," a monthly periodical conducted by his friend, Lewis Gaylord Clark, all of them such as he only could write. They were afterward collected into a volume, entitled "Wolfert's Roost," from the ancient name of that beautiful residence of his on the banks of the Hudson, in which they were mostly written. They were, perhaps, read with more interest in the volume than in the magazine, just as some paintings of the highest merit are seen with more pleasure in the artist's room than on the walls of an exhibition.

In 1842, he went to Spain as the American minister, and remained in that country for four years. I have never understood that anything occurred during that time to put his talents as a negotiator to any rigorous test. He was a sagacious and intelligent observer; his connection with the American Legation in London had given him diplomatic experience, and I have heard that he sent home to his government some valuable despatches on the subject of our relations with Spain. In other respects, he did, at least, what all American ministers at the European courts are doing, and I suppose my hearers understand very well what that is ; but if there had been any question of importance to be settled, I think he might have acquitted himself as well as many who have had a higher reputation for dexterity in business. When I was at Madrid in 1857, a distinguished Spaniard said to me : "Why does not your government send out Washington Irving to this court ? Why do you not take as your agent the man whom all Spain admires, venerates, loves ? I assure you, it would be difficult for our government to refuse anything which Irving should ask, and his signature would make almost any treaty acceptable to our people."

Returning in 1846, Irving went back to Sunnyside, on the

Hudson, and continued to make it his abode for the rest of his life. Those who passed up and down the river before the year 1835, may remember a neglected cottage on a green bank, with a few locust-trees before it, close to where a little brook brings in its tribute to the mightier stream. In that year Irving became its possessor ; he gave it the name it now wears, planted its pleasant slopes with trees and shrubs, laid it out in walks, built outhouses, and converted the cottage into a more spacious dwelling, in the old Dutch style of architecture, with crow-steps on the gables ; a quaint, picturesque building, with " as many angles and corners," to use his own words, " as a cocked hat." He caused creeping plants and climbing roses to be trained up its walls ; the trees he planted prospered in that sheltered situation, and were filled with birds, which would not leave their nests at the approach of the kind master of the place. The house became almost hidden from sight by their lofty summits, the perpetual rustlings of which, to those who sat within, were blended with the murmurs cf the water. Van Tassel would have had some difficulty in recognizing his old abode in this little paradise, with the beauty of which one of Irving's friends * has made the public familiar in prose and verse.

At Sunnyside, Irving wrote his " Life of Oliver Goldsmith." Putnam, the bookseller, had said to him one day : " Here is Foster's ' Life of Goldsmith ;' I think of republishing it." " I once wrote a Memoir of Goldsmith," answered Irving, " which was prefixed to an edition of his works printed at Paris ; and I have thought of enlarging it and making it more perfect." " If you will do that," was the reply of the bookseller, " I shall not republish the Life by Foster." Within three months afterward,

* H. T. Tuckerman.

Irving's "Life of Goldsmith" was finished and in press. It was so much superior to the original sketch, in the exactness of the particulars, the entertainment of the anecdotes, and the beauty of the style, that it was really a new work. For my part, I know of nothing like it. I have read no biographical memoir which carries forward the reader so delightfully and with so little tediousness of recital or reflection. I never take it up without being tempted to wish that Irving had written more works of the kind; but this could hardly be ; for where could he have found another Goldsmith ?

In 1850, appeared his "Lives of Mahomet and his Successors," composed principally from memoranda made by him during his residence in Spain; and in the same year he completed the revisal of his works for a new edition, which was brought out by Putnam, a bookseller of whose obliging and honorable conduct he delighted to speak. Irving was a man with whom it was not easy to have a misunderstanding ; but, even if he had been of a different temper, these commendations would have been none the less deserved.

When Cooper died, toward the close of the year 1850, Irving, who had not long before met him, apparently in the full vigor of his excellent constitution, was much shocked by the event, and took part in the meetings held for the purpose of collecting funds to erect a monument to his memory in this city—a design which, I am sorry to say, has wholly failed. He wrote a letter advising that the monument should be a statue, and attended the great memorial meeting held in Metropolitan Hall, in February of the next year, at which Webster presided. He was then near the end of his sixty-eighth year, and was remarked as one over whom the last twenty years had passed lightly. He, whom Dr. Francis describes as in early life a slender and delicate

youth, preserving his health by habitual daily exercise, appeared
before that vast assembly a fresh, well-preserved gentleman
scarcely more than elderly, with firm but benevolent features,
well-knit and muscular limbs, and an elastic step, the sign of un-
diminished physical vigor.

In his retirement at Sunnyside, Irving planned and executed
his last great work, the "Life of Washington," to which he says
he had long looked forward as his crowning literary effort.   Constable, the Edinburgh bookseller, had proposed it to him thirty
years before, and he then resolved to undertake it as soon as he
should return to the United States.   It was postponed in favor
of other projects, but never abandoned.   At length the expected
time seemed to have arrived ; his other tasks had been successfully performed ; the world was waiting for new works from his
pen ; his mind and body were yet in their vigor; the habit and
the love of literary production yet remained, and he addressed
himself to this greatest of his labors.

Yet he had his misgivings, though they could not divert him
from his purpose.   "They expect too much—too much," he said
to a friend of mine, to whom he was speaking of the magnitude
of the task and the difficulty of satisfying the public.   We cannot wonder at these doubts.   At the time when he began to
employ himself steadily on this work, he was near the age of
threescore and ten, when with most men the season of hope and
confidence is past.   He was like one who should begin the great
labor of the day when the sun was shedding his latest beams,
and what if the shadows of night should descend upon him before his task was ended ?   A vast labor had been thrown upon
him by the almost numberless documents and papers recently
brought to light relating to the events in which Washington was
concerned—such as were amassed and digested by the research

of Sparks, and accompanied by the commentary of his excellent biography. These were all to be carefully examined and their spirit extracted. Historians had in the meantime arisen in our country, of a world-wide fame, with whose works his own must be compared, and he was to be judged by a public whom he, more than almost any other man, had taught to be impatient of mediocrity.

I do not believe, however, that Irving's task would have been performed so ably if it had been undertaken when it was suggested by Constable ; the narrative could not have been so complete in its facts ; it might not have been written with the same becoming simplicity. It was fortunate that the work was delayed till it could be written from the largest store of materials, till its plan was fully matured in all its fair proportions, and till the author's mind had become filled with the profoundest veneration for his subject.

The simplicity already mentioned is the first quality of this work which impresses the reader. Here is a man of genius, a poet by temperament, writing the life of a man of transcendent wisdom and virtue—a life passed amidst great events, and marked by inestimable public services. There is a constant temptation to eulogy, but the temptation is resisted ; the actions of his hero are left to speak their own praise. He records events reverently, as one might have recorded them before the art of rhetoric was invented, with no exaggeration, with no parade of reflection ; the lessons of the narrative are made to impress themselves on the mind by the earnest and conscientious relation of facts. Meantime the narrator keeps himself in the background, solely occupied with the due presentation of his subject. Our eyes are upon the actors whom he sets before us—we never think of Mr. Irving.

A closer examination reveals another great merit of the work, the admirable proportion in which the author keeps the characters and events of his story. I suppose he could hardly have been conscious of this merit, and that it was attained without a direct effort. Long meditation had probably so shaped and matured the plan in his mind, and so arranged its parts in their just symmetry, that, executing it as he did, conscientiously, he could not have made it a different thing from what we have it. There is nothing distorted, nothing placed in too broad a light or thrown too far in the shade. The incidents of our Revolutionary war, the great event of Washington's life, pass before us as they passed before the eyes of the commander-in-chief himself, and from time to time varied his designs. Washington is kept always in sight, and the office of the biographer is never allowed to become merged in that of the historian.

The men who were the companions of Washington in the field or in civil life, are shown only in their association with him, yet are their characters drawn, not only with skill and spirit, but with a hand that delighted to do them justice. Nothing, I believe, could be more abhorrent to Irving's ideas of the province of a biographer, than the slightest detraction from the merits of others, that his hero might appear the more eminent. So remarkable is his work in this respect, that an accomplished member of the Historical Society,* who has analyzed the merits of the " Life of Washington" with a critical skill which makes me ashamed to speak of the work after him, has declared that no writer, within the circle of his reading, " has so successfully established his claim to the rare and difficult virtue of impartiality."

I confess, my admiration of this work becomes the greater the

---

* G. W. Greene. " Biographical Studies."

more I examine it. In the other writings of Irving are beauties which strike the reader at once. In this I recognize qualities which lie deeper, and which I was not sure of finding—a rare equity of judgment, a large grasp of the subject, a profound philosophy, independent of philosophical forms, and even instinctively rejecting them, the power of reducing an immense crowd of loose materials to clear and orderly arrangement, and forming them into one grand whole, as a skillful commander, from a rabble of raw recruits, forms a disciplined army, animated and moved by a single will.

The greater part of this last work of Irving was composed while he was in the enjoyment of what might be called a happy old age. This period of his life was not without its infirmities, but his frame was yet unwasted, his intellect bright and active, and the hour of decay seemed distant. He had become more than ever the object of public veneration, and in his beautiful retreat enjoyed all the advantages with few of the molestations of acknowledged greatness ; a little too much visited, perhaps, but submitting to the intrusion of his admirers with his characteristic patience and kindness. That retreat had now become more charming than ever, and the domestic life within was as beautiful as the nature without. A surviving brother, older than himself, shared it with him, and several affectionate nephews and nieces stood to him in the relation of sons and daughters. He was surrounded by neighbors who saw him daily, and honored and loved him the more for knowing him so well.

While he was engaged in writing the last pages of his " Life of Washington," his countrymen heard with pain that his health was failing and his strength ebbing away. He completed the work, however, though he was not able to revise the last sheets, and we then heard that his nights had become altogether sleepless. He was himself of opinion that his labors had been too severe for his time of life, and had sometimes feared that the power to continue them would desert him before his work could be finished. A catarrh to which he had been subject, had, by some injudicious prescription, been converted into an asthma, and the asthma, according to the testimony of his physician, Dr. Peters, one of the most attentive and assiduous of his profession, was at length accompanied by an enlargement of the heart. This disease ended in the usual way by a sudden dissolution. On the 28th of November last, in the evening, he had bidden the family good night in his usual kind manner, and had withdrawn to his room, attended by one of his nieces carrying his medicines, when he complained of a sudden feeling of intense sadness, sank immediately into her arms, and died without a struggle.

Although he had reached an age beyond which life is rarely prolonged, the news of his death was everywhere received with profound sorrow. The whole country mourned, but the grief was most deeply felt in his immediate neighborhood ; the little children wept for the loss of their good friend. When the day of his funeral arrived, the people gathered from far and near to attend it ; this capital poured fourth its citizens ; the trains on the railway were crowded, and a multitude, like a mass meeting, but reverentially silent, moved through the streets of the neighboring village, which had been dressed in the emblems of mourning, and clustered about the church and the burial-ground. It was the first day of December ; the pleasant Indian summer of our climate had been prolonged far beyond its usual date ; the sun shone with his softest splendor and the elements were hushed into a perfect calm ; it was like one of the blandest days of October. The hills and forests, the meadows and waters which

Irving had loved seemed listening, in that quiet atmosphere, as the solemn funeral service was read.

It was read over the remains of one whose life had well prepared his spirit for its new stage of being. Irving did not aspire to be a theologian, but his heart was deeply penetrated with the better part of religion, and he had sought humbly to imitate the example of the Great Teacher of our faith.

That amiable character which makes itself so manifest in the writings of Irving was seen in all his daily actions. He was ever ready to do kind offices, tender of the feelings of others, carefully just, but ever leaning to the merciful side of justice, averse from strife, and so modest that the world never ceased to wonder how it should have happened that one so much praised should have gained so little assurance. He envied no man's success, he sought to detract from no man's merits, but he was acutely sensitive both to praise and to blame—sensitive to such a degree that an unfavorable criticism of any of his works would almost persuade him that they were as worthless as the critic represented them. He thought so little of himself that he could never comprehend why it was that he should be the object of curiosity or reverence.

From the time that he began the composition of his " Sketch Book," his whole life was the life of an author. His habits of composition were, however, by no means regular. When he was in the vein, the periods would literally stream from his pen; at other times he would scarcely write anything. For two years after the failure of his brothers at Liverpool, he found it almost impossible to write a line. He was throughout life an early riser, and when in the mood, would write all the morning and till late in the day, wholly engrossed with his subject. In the evening he was ready for any cheerful pastime, in which he took part with an animation almost amounting to high spirits. These intervals of excitement and intense labor, sometimes lasting for weeks, were succeeded by languor, and at times by depression of spirits, and for months the pen would lie untouched; even to answer a letter at these times was an irksome task.

In the evening he wrote but very rarely, knowing—so, at least, I infer—that no habit makes severer demands upon the nervous system than this. It was owing, I doubt not, to this prudent husbanding of his powers, along with his somewhat abstinent habits and the exercise which he took every day, that he was able to preserve unimpaired to so late a period the faculties employed in original composition. He has been a vigorous walker and a fearless rider, and in his declining years he drove out daily, not only for the sake of the open air and motion, but to refresh his mind with the aspect of nature. One of his favorite recreations was listening to music, of which he was an indulgent critic, and he contrived to be pleased and soothed by strains less artfully modulated than fastidious ears are apt to require.

His facility in writing and the charm of his style were owing to very early practice, the reading of good authors and the native elegance of his mind, and not, in my opinion, to any special study of the graces of manner or any anxious care in the use of terms and phrases. Words and combinations of words are sometimes found in his writings to which a fastidious taste might object ; but these do not prevent his style from being one of the most agreeable in the whole range of our literature. It is transparent as the light, sweetly modulated, unaffected, the native expression of a fertile fancy, a benignant temper, and a mind which, delighting in the noble and the beautiful, turned involuntarily away from their opposites. His peculiar humor was, in a great measure, the offspring of this constitution of his

mind. This "fanciful playing with common things," as Mr.
Dana calls it, is never coarse, never tainted with grossness, and
always in harmony with our better sympathies. It not only
tinged his writings, but overflowed in his delightful conversation.

I have thus set before you, my friends, with such measure of
ability as I possess, a rapid and imperfect sketch of the life, character and genius of Washington Irving. Other hands will yet
give the world a bolder, more vivid and more exact portraiture.
In the meantime, when I consider for how many years he stood
before the world as an author, with a still increasing fame—half
a century in this most changeful of centuries—I cannot hesitate
to predict for him a deathless renown. Since he began to write,
empires have risen and passed away ; mighty captains have
appeared on the stage of the world, performed their part, and
been called to their account ; wars have been fought and ended,
which have changed the destinies of the human race. New arts
have been invented and adopted, and have pushed the old out of
use ; the household economy of half mankind has undergone a
revolution. Science has learned a new dialect and forgotten the
old ; the chemist of 1807 would be a vain babbler among his
brethren of the present day, and would in turn become bewil-
dered in the attempt to understand them. Nation utters speech
to nation in words that pass from realm to realm with the speed
of light. Distant countries have been made neighbors ; the
Atlantic Ocean has become a narrow frith, and the Old World
and the New shake hands across it ; the East and the West
look in at each other's windows. The new inventions bring
new calamities, and men perish in crowds by the recoil of their
own devices. War has learned more frightful modes of havoc,
and armed himself with deadlier weapons ; armies are borne to
the battle-field on the wings of the wind, and dashed against

each other and destroyed with infinite bloodshed. We grow giddy with this perpetual whirl of strange events, these rapid and ceaseless mutations ; the earth seems to reel under our feet, and we turn to those who write like Irving, for some assurance that we are still in the same world into which we were born ; we read, and are quieted and consoled. In his pages we see that the language of the heart never becomes obsolete ; that Truth and Good and Beauty, the offspring of God, are not subject to the changes which beset the inventions of men. We become satisfied that he whose works were the delight of our fathers, and are still ours, will be read with the same pleasure by those who come after us.

If it were becoming, at this time and in this assembly, to address our departed friend as if in his immediate presence, I would say : "Farewell, thou who hast entered into the rest prepared, from the foundation of the world, for serene and gentle spirits like thine. Farewell, happy in thy life, happy in thy death, happier in the reward to which that death was the assured passage ; fortunate in attracting the admiration of the world to thy beautiful writings ; still more fortunate in having written nothing which did not tend to promote the reign of magnanimous forbearance and generous sympathies among thy fellow-men. The brightness of that enduring fame which thou hast won on earth is but a shadowy symbol of the glory to which thou art admitted in the world beyond the grave. Thy errand upon earth was an errand of peace and good-will to men, and thou art now in a region where hatred and strife never enter, and where the harmonious activity of those who inhabit it acknowledges no impulse less noble or less pure than that of love."